REFLECTIONS OF
Neath &
Port Talbot

REFLECTIONS OF
Neath &
Port Talbot

BY DAVID ROBERTS

Courier

breedon **books**
PUBLISHING

First published in Great Britain in 2002 by
The Breedon Books Publishing Company Limited
Breedon House, 3 The Parker Centre,
Derby, DE21 4SZ.

ISBN 1 85983 333 0

Printed and bound by Butler & Tanner, Frome, Somerset, England.

Cover printing by Lawrence-Allen Colour Printers, Weston-super-Mare, Somerset, England.

CONTENTS

AN APPRECIATION

This book would not have been possible without the valued assistance of the many residents of the towns of Neath and Port Talbot who submitted their individual images of days gone by, especially readers of the *Neath & Port Talbot Courier* newspapers. Particular thanks are due to:

Cheryl Roberts
Grace and Robert Thomas
Byron Sambrook
Keith and Ann Davies
Ivor Speed
Bill Adams
Lindsey & Gaynor Davies
Graham & Linda James
Roy & Elsie Wilcox,
Peter & the late G.V. Knowles
Malcolm Dummer
Janet Jones
Peter Lloyd
Malcolm Gullam
Annette Jones, Robert Merrill and Claire Roberts
Neath & Port Talbot Museums and Libraries Service
Susan Beckley & Kim Collis, West Glamorgan Archive Service
Kay Harris, Norman Reed
John Vivian Hughes
John Southard and Tony Crocker

FOREWORD

LEAFING through the picture-packed pages of *Reflections of Neath & Port Talbot* will be a remarkable experience for many. Perhaps even more notable is that it is the fourth such book in a successful series to appear in consecutive years.

Accomplishing that task could have presented anything other than an easy task, but once again David Roberts has succeeded in gathering an interesting array of images from days gone by.

Reflections of Neath & Port Talbot follows in the footsteps of books which have each made their own significant contribution to recording days past in the two towns. It continues to reap a rich harvest of memories from within the community and in doing so performs many functions. Most important perhaps is that it draws together pictures, which might otherwise be lost to the community archive.

These each tell their individual story, but added together combine for an unforgettable tale. By now more than 1600 images have been brought together for an album to be shared by all. *The Courier* is proud to be associated with such an evocative and unique publication.

George Edwards,
Editorial Director
Neath & Port Talbot Courier newspapers

STAGING POSTS ON THE ROUTE OF HISTORY

MANY people will say that the towns of Neath and Port Talbot each have their own distinct identity. This may be true, but they also share many clear similarities. Not least in recent times has been the speed with which change has been thrust among their proud communities.

Both towns have endured much that revolutions agricultural, industrial and now technological, have brought with them. Both have acquitted themselves well.

The towns also share a rich and varied history, that can be traced back much further than these landmarks. They have links with Celtic times when the hillsides at Margam and Briton Ferry underlined the importance of the coastal route to West Wales.

While Neath was an important staging post for the advance of the Roman Conquest, the Borough of Aberavon can trace its lineage back to mediaeval times with the granting of its charter in the early 14th century.

And though the Cistercian abbeys at Margam and Neath with their vast estates served to dominate early social and economic life, the arrival of the Industrial Revolution made a far greater impact.

While copper smelting at Aberdulais marks its earliest development it was the need for iron and coal for works and transport that brought the transformation of the towns into what for many people will be most familiar. It was a transformation that carried the names of Neath and Port Talbot around the world. It was also one that brought with it a need for social change.

Urban development has pushed out from the serried ranks of terraced homes common to the centres of both towns. This created new communities as it swallowed up once green, wide-open spaces. In Port Talbot, the sprawling estates at Sandfields and Baglan are prime examples, while Neath can offer those at Cimla and Bryncoch.

Each one of the people who live there and indeed throughout the rest of the County Borough will have their own particular memories of days gone by. The photographs within the pages of this book will evoke many more.

In that, it is perhaps an album that turns the communities it reflects into one big family.

David Roberts
2002

STREET LIFE

The Gwyn Hall, Orchard Street, Neath, with the statue of its main benefactor Howell Gwyn outside, 1898. The statue is no longer there, standing instead just inside the entrance to nearby Victoria Gardens.

Water Street, Aberavon, looking towards High Street, 1900. W.J. Williams, Cloth Hall, with some of its wares displayed outside is on the right.

Queen Street, Neath, 1900. On the left can be seen Jones Borough stores, from where, back to the camera, the Marks & Spencer store now stands.

Tydraw Hill, Port Talbot 1900. The bridge, long since removed, carried the Port Talbot Railway and Docks freight line. The larger building looking down on the scene is Saron Chapel. Alongside, the terraced cottages were originally the homes of railway workers.

Looking along Windsor Road, Neath, 1900.

The Prince of Wales Hotel on the corner of Water Street, Aberavon, 1904. The road had yet to become one of the worst traffic bottlenecks anywhere in South Wales, a situation that remained until the opening of the M4 motorway in 1965.

Hutchins Medical Hall, Queen Street, Neath, is where many sought relief for their ailments in the early 1900s.

The Square, Neath, early 1900s, showing the tower of St Thomas Parish Church behind.

The huge lamps which hung outside meant there was no mistaking the millinery and drapery shop known as R.Davies' Temple of Fashion in High Street, Aberavon, 1903.

Lower Station Road, Port Talbot, with the Grand Hotel in the distance, 1910.

Green Street, Neath, 1900. The days of multiple stores with their bright lights had yet to dawn.

Lower Water Street, Aberavon, with the rooftop of Cloth Hall in the background, 1910.

Springfield Terrace, just off Briton Ferry Road, Neath, in the early 1900s before Neath Methodist Chapel – the so-called Penny Brick chapel – was built in front. The decorations on the houses indicate that some kind of celebration was under way.

E. Cook's drapery, Mansel Street, Port Talbot, 1910.

Orchard Street, Neath, 1907. One of the town's gas trams heads away from the camera.

High Street, Aberavon, with a policeman on point duty, 1930s.

The Laurels, Lewis Road, Neath, with its extensive railed gardens, early 1900s.

A. & G. Viazzani's, Water Street, Aberavon, retail tobacconists and refreshment bar with its express tea and coffee service was a regular meeting place to exchange local gossip. This picture was taken in the mid-1930s.

New Street, Neath, looking down towards the Castle Hotel, 1908.

A wet winter's day in Upper Water Street, Aberavon, 1950. The County furnishing store is on the right hand side.

The Square, Neath, 1908. New Street disappears into the left of the photograph.

High Street, Aberavon, showing The Walnut Tree Hotel on the left and the Maypole grocery store in the centre, along with Cash & Co, and Burton Tailoring on the right, September, 1950.

Neath station forecourt, 1910.

The Bon Marche store, of tailors, hatters and outfitters, Thomas H. Hawkins, Green Street, Neath, 1910. It was instantly recognisable by the pair of cast-iron lions that stood guard at either side of the elevated shop front.

The sight of the motorway marching across Port Talbot on stilts was welcome for many in 1963, but it would be a while before the town's traffic chaos would vanish completely for the motorway didn't open until 1965.

Queen Street, Neath, looking down towards Green Street and the town's market, 1910.

A Thomas Bros bus turns to head into the centre of Port Talbot around Wern Chapel, 1966. Much traffic had been taken away from the town by the opening a year earlier of the A48(M), now the M4 motorway. The chapel was demolished in 1972.

A view across Port Talbot from the mountainside above Penycae, 1954. In the distance can be seen the rapidly expanding Sandfields estate which helped to house the influx of men seeking work in the town's new giant steelworks.

Briton Ferry Road, Neath, 1910. The buildings on the centre right are now a social club. The tramlines used by Neath's gas trams are very much in evidence.

Upper Water Street, Aberavon, 1967, showing the Walnut Tree Hotel and some of the shops demolished to make way for town centre redevelopment.

A 1911 view of Victoria Gardens, Neath. The Gnoll House can be seen among the trees in the upper centre of the picture.

High Street, Aberavon, looking towards the motorway flyover. The picture was taken on April 6, 1967 and the shops on the left hand side demolished less than a year later.

London Road, Neath, looking towards Orchard Street, 1935. The horse is emerging from Alfred Street and Victoria Gardens is behind the railings on the right. The gardens had yet to be cut back to make way for the bus station which bears its name.

Talbot Square, Aberavon – often referred to as Cwmavon Square – July, 1967. This was another commercial area swallowed up by redevelopment.

A shopper hurries along Queen Street, Neath, with its busy collection of small shops, 1940s.

High Street, Aberavon,
looking eastwards
towards the Walnut Tree
Hotel, 1967. On the right
is Lloyds Bank and next
to it the former Grand
Cinema, by then a bingo
hall.

Orchard Street, Neath,
1940s.

Clarence Street,
Aberavon, 1970. It was
demolished soon after
to make way for town
centre redevelopment.

Orchard Street, Neath, early 1950s. The building with the advertising hoarding has long since been demolished and today serves as a car park at the back of the town's Marks & Spencer store.

The David Evans store, High Street, Aberavon, shortly before demolition, 1970s. The building was formerly a cinema. On the right can be seen Walnut Tree Lane.

Who says our weather isn't like it used to be? Days of storms and torrential rain caused Neath's Gnoll brook to overflow on July 18, 1955, sending millions of gallons of water flooding into the town centre. This was the scene at the eastern end of London Road.

The cattle market at the corner of Green Street and The Parade, Neath in the early 1950s. The Full Moon public house and Dorothy Hotel can be seen behind, while the Market Tavern is on the right.

Clearance work under way in 1972 at the top of Lower Water Street, Aberavon, in preparation for the town centre redevelopment that was to follow.

The old meets the new. Looking down the lane that led from Talbot Square on to High Street, Aberavon, captured as work proceeds apace on the new Aberafan Centre, in the background, 1973.

This raised floral display celebrating the work of Civil Defence volunteers was an eye-catching feature of Victoria Gardens, Neath, during one early 1950s spring and summer.

Initial building work on the Aberafan Centre, Port Talbot, with the roof of the town's old market visible behind, along with the tower of St Mary's Parish Church, 1973.

The roundabout at Stockham's Corner, Neath, was bursting with flowers when this 1966 picture, looking down Windsor Road, was taken. Many of the properties on the left and right, were demolished to make way for the entry of Neath's Southern relief link road in the early 1970s.

A unique view of the interior of the Aberafan Shopping Centre mall square, during its construction, 1975.

Florence Street, Neath, 1966. It was later demolished to make way for the town's Southern link road.

Many would say it had taken a long time, but by 1975, as this aerial view shows, work was well advanced on development of Port Talbot's new town centre buildings.

King Street, Neath, 1966. The Oxford Hotel still stands today, but many of the buildings in this picture vanished to make way for the town's Southern link road.

Talbot Road, Port Talbot, near the Abbey Road traffic light junction, 1980.

The Eastland Road, Neath, depot of the South Wales Transport Company on February 28, 1971, the day it closed its doors to buses for the last time. It was later taken over by the South Wales Electricity Board before finally being demolished to make way for new housing.

Victoria Gardens bus station, Neath, 1973.

The back entrance of the Aberavon Shopping Centre, Port Talbot, during winter 1982.

Talbot Road, Port Talbot, with the Plaza Cinema just visible on the left, 1982.

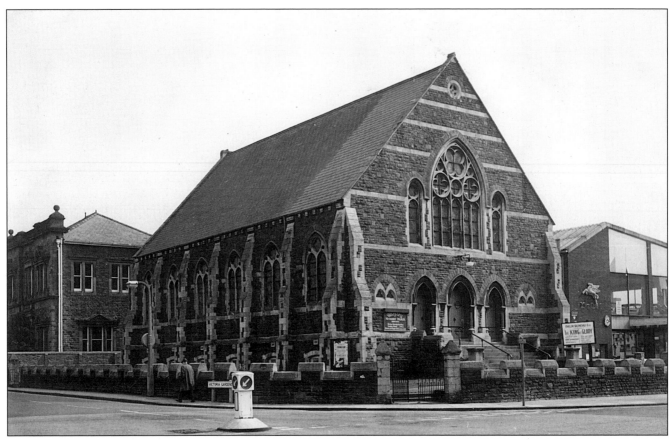

Wesley Methodist Chapel, Neath, 1975. The building was demolished soon after and the site is now occupied by a doctors, surgery and sheltered housing complex.

Station Road, Port Talbot, 1982.

Upper Station Road, Port Talbot, 1985.

Across the rooftops of Neath – a view captured in 1984, from the Cimla Court Hotel. Bryncoch is in the background.

A 1976 bird's-eye view of Neath town centre.

FAMILIAR FACES

This was the crowd that solemnly gathered near Port Talbot General station on August 12, 1914, to say farewell to members of the Royal Horse Artillery, off to fight in the First World War.

Skewen Salvation Army Corps Songster Brigade, with corps officers, 1932.

A group of friends from Cwmavon, pose for one for the album, Thursday, June 14, 1923.

The 3rd Neath Scout troop and Cub pack with scoutmaster Cliff Bartlett, 1932.

Time to relax for this elderly Port Talbot couple in the far-off days of the late 1930s.

Metal Box staff at a dinner and dance at the Castle Hotel, Neath, 1939, shortly after the outbreak of the Second World War.

Bryn Whist Club, Port Talbot, 1937.

The Neath Busmen's Welfare Club and Sports Institute stewardess, officers and committee, 1944.

Bethany Chapel elders, Port Talbot, 1940s.

Neath Labour Party Women's section held a children's Christmas party – attended by Father Christmas of course – in 1947.

The late 1940s were definitely a time for reflection for young Ian Lewis and his Afan Valley grandad Ben Lewis, pictured strolling down a country lane.

The Young Peoples, Singing Company of Skewen Salvation Army Corps, 1948.

A meeting of the Welfare Foods Campaign Wales region, took place at the Masonic Hall, Forge Road, Port Talbot, on September 27, 1950. Apart from the mothers and children, also present were: front, left to right: Mr E.R. Brett, district food executive officer; Miss E.G. Wright, county superintendent of health visitors; Councillor Richard Evans, deputy mayor; Councillor Mrs T.I. Rees, mayoress of Port Talbot; Mrs V. Beavis, secretary of the WVS; Nurse Olive Davies, health visitor. Back row: Mr A.J. Adsley, centre, officer in charge of Port Talbot food office.

A gathering of members of Briton Ferry Little Theatre, early 1960s.

A lads' night out at Taibach Rugby Club, Port Talbot, 1953.

Buffet time at a Neath Co-op social, 1950.

All dressed up to celebrate, this group of women worked at the main staff canteen at the Steel Company of Wales, Port Talbot. They are pictured at The Walnut Tree hotel, Water Street, Aberavon, in July, 1958 celebrating the retirement of their supervisor Mrs Griffiths.

Neath neighbours from Duck Street, Castle Buildings, Glamorgan Street and Castle Street, joined together with residents of Cattle Street for a party to celebrate the Festival of Britain, on August 28, 1951. The woman with the flowers was Mrs Gomer Richards, owner of a grocery shop in Cattle Street. The only man in the group is her son, also named Gomer.

Staff of the Woolworth's store at Station Road, Port Talbot, during an early 1960s Christmas party.

Briton Ferry Retained Fire-fighters at their 1952 social.

A group of regulars at Velindre Social Club, Port Talbot, early 1960s.

Party time for children of Briton Ferry's retained firemen, 1952.

A night out for staff of the Steel Company of Wales central engineering shop, Christmas 1962 at The York Hotel, Bridgend.

Patrons of the Crown Inn, Briton Ferry, July, 1952.

Members of the civil engineering department of the Steel Company of Wales, Port Talbot, at a dinner in the works canteen, late 1960s.

Neighbours of Illtyd Street, Neath, gather for a street party to celebrate the Coronation of Queen Elizabeth II, June, 1953.

Members of Cwmavon Brownie pack with their leaders, 1966.

Labour councillors at the Aberavon seafront temporary offices of Port Talbot Borough Council, early 1970s.

Patients at Cymla hospital, Neath, get together to celebrate Christmas, 1955.

Neath Post Office staff at a 1955 party.

Governors of Dyffryn Comprehensive School, Margam, Port Talbot, mid-1970s.

Children of employees of South Wales Transport's Eastland Road, Neath, depot at their Christmas party at the neighbouring British Legion Club, 1956.

Members of Cwmavon Ward Labour Party women's section in the mid-1970s in the seafront office of the Mayor of the Borough of Afan.

Members of Neath Municipal Choir, 1958, with the Borough Mayor, Alderman W.S. Atkins.

Officers and guests at Neath Cricket Club's annual dinner and dance at The Castle Hotel, Neath, 1963.

Plumbers from Neath and Port Talbot gathered at Briton Ferry Rugby and Cricket Club for an annual dinner, late-1960s.

Briton Ferry Brownies turned out to salute Falklands War hero Richard Chapel of Hengwrt, Briton Ferry, when he returned home from the campaign in 1982.

A final get-together for some of the engineering workers at the South Wales Transport bus company depot at Neath Abbey, formerly the Western Welsh depot, August, 1984.

The class of 1976 at the Sanderson School of Dancing, Port Talbot.

Members of Aslam Sewing Guild at their meeting at St David's Church Hall, Neath, mid-1950s.

Members of Cimla, Neath, Beaver pack, in their Cimla Crescent headquarters, 1989.

AROUND THE DISTRICTS

High Street, Taibach, Port Talbot, 1910.

The bridge across the River Neath at Resolven, in the early 1900s. It linked the village with the main Neath Valley road.

Ynysygwas bridge, Cwmavon, late 1930s.

Commercial Road, Resolven, early 1900s.

Whitford Cottage, Baglan, 1930s. It later fell into ruin and was eventually bulldozed with the construction of BP Chemicals' Baglan Bay petro-chemical complex.

Bethania Chapel, Skewen, 1909.

The original Miners' Arms, Old Road, Skewen, 1910.

Houses at the entrance to Ladies' Walk, Baglan, late 1940s. This is now Thorney Road.

A view across Cwmavon from 'the top road', 1942.

St Catherine's Church, Melyncrythan, Neath, 1912.

The park, Cwmavon, early 1950s.

The centre of Bryncoch, Neath, 1912. The store on the left became the village Post Office.

Margam Road, Margam, looking towards Port Talbot, 1955.

High Street, Glynneath, 1914.

Roadworks at the junction of Albion Road, Mayberry Road and Crawford Road, Baglan, Port Talbot, in the mid-1950s. The houses being built are those in Crawford Green, and behind them Thorney Road.

Neath Road, Briton Ferry, 1914, viewed eastwards from the railway bridge that once crossed the road at this point. The Crown Inn is the white-washed building on the left.

Road surfacing work under way at Mayberry Road, Baglan, Port Talbot, shortly after the houses along it were built, mid-1950s.

The view up New Road, Skewen, 1920s.

Construction work under way on the council houses and roadway at Hawthorn Avenue, Baglan, Port Talbot, mid-1950s.

Asher 'Harry' Crocker outside the Villiers café, which he ran at Villiers Street, Briton Ferry, in the 1920s. Alongside him is his wife Catherine. He was also known as Harry the milk because he had his own dairy behind the café.

Aberavon Beach, looking towards Swansea, during the late 1950s.

Cwrt Sart railway station, Briton Ferry, in September 1921 and shows the stationmaster and members of his staff.

The Public Hall, at Neath Road, Briton Ferry, was opened in 1911 and demolished in 1969. In its time it was used as a theatre, ballroom, cinema and a venue for political meetings. The site later became a filling station and is now occupied by a car sales showroom. This picture was taken during the 1920s when the building was in use as a cinema.

Hard to believe today perhaps, but in 1954 this was the view up the Goytre Valley, just north of Dyffryn locomotive depot, Taibach, Port Talbot. The railway headed up towards Bryn and Maesteg.

The view seawards across Taibach, Port Talbot, in 1954. It shows the cemetery at Chapel of Ease on the right and the busy Dyffryn railway marshalling yard, now developed for housing, on the left.

Looking down New Road, Skewen, 1926, the year of the General Strike.

Straight as a die – that is the main Swansea to Paddington railway line and the A48(M) now both joined by the M4 motorway as they stretch across Baglan Moors. Much housing and industrial development has changed this early 1960s scene almost beyond recognition.

A late 1940s view of the eastern edge of Briton Ferry. The area changed dramatically with the construction of Briton Ferry viaduct. The roundabout now occupies much of the area in the centre of the picture. The area around the hut in the foreground is now occupied by a McDonald's fast food drive-in restaurant.

Cavalli's transport café near Briton Ferry roundabout, early 1950s. The Travellers' Rest public house can be seen behind.

Cefn Parc, near Llandarcy, Skewen, early 1950s.

The famous Beulah Round Chapel, at Groes village, Margam, Port Talbot, in the late 1960s. It was soon to be dismantled stone-by-stone and rebuilt in nearby Tollgate Park, to make way for the march eastwards of the M4 motorway. The village and its school were not so lucky. They were demolished.

Canalside, Aberdulais in the early 1950s.

The pier at Aberavon Beach and distant stone breakwater, with a Thomas Bros bus in the foreground, 1966.

The Ivy Tower, Tonna, with an ivy-clad Danylan farmhouse below, early 1950s.

The remains of a railway bridge at Pontrhydyfen, early 1960s. The parapets were later removed to widen the road and relieve the hazard presented to traffic at this point.

Foundations of a bungalow in Butler's field, Cimla Common, 1952. Crynallt House can be seen in the background.

The library, at Laurel Avenue, Baglan, Port Talbot, pictured soon after it opened its doors for the first time on May 4, 1967. New housing development can be seen proceeding apace behind.

Cimla Road, Cimla, Neath, in the early 1950s. The Cimla Hotel can clearly be seen, but the open space on the left hand side had yet to be developed as a filling station, rugby club and the Church of Saints Peter and Paul. Today a supermarket occupies much of the site.

An early 1970s view of Baglan, Port Talbot, showing the housing estate, and below it the Baglan dual carriageway, once one of the most heavily trafficked roads in Wales.

A view across the rooftops of Briton Ferry, 1953. The town's railway station can be seen in the centre.

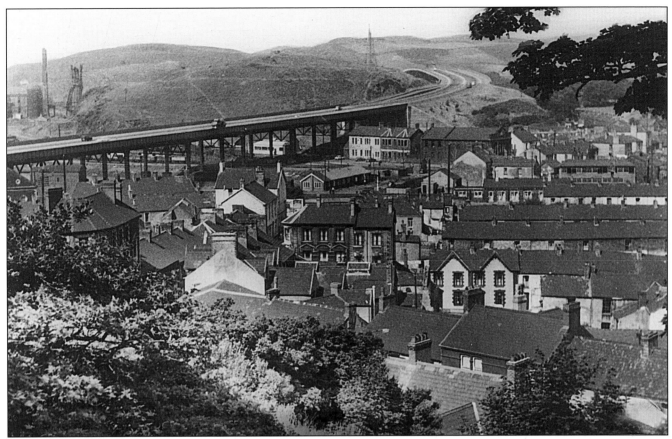

Briton Ferry, shortly after the opening of Briton Ferry viaduct and Neath river bridge, in 1955.

Chain Road housing development, Glynneath, mid-1950s.

The railway bridge at the eastern end of Commercial Road, Taibach, 1972. It was removed in May, 1973.

A view of Briton Ferry, its redundant dock and basin, 1965. Also visible is the Duport steelworks, formerly the Albion steelworks.

A United Welsh bus heads across Cimla common, Neath, bound for Swansea from Blaengwynfi, 1969.

Velindre and Penycae, Port Talbot, looking seawards, 1979. The industrial area in the centre of the photograph has now been redeveloped for housing.

An aerial view of housing development at Cimla, Neath, September, 1983.

The Grand Hotel, Station Road, Port Talbot, provides the backdrop for this view of a military procession through the town shortly after the First World War.

A Whitsun procession of Neath churchgoers along the town's Windsor Road, 1920s.

A Port Talbot wedding, 1915. The groom was Herbert Speed and his blushing bride, Gertrude Williams. The background is probably No.1 Saron Cottages.

Celebrating the Coronation of King George VI at Park Drive, Skewen, 1937.

The people of Corlanau, Port Talbot, gather to celebrate the Coronation of King George VI, 1937.

Part of the VE Day celebrations at Henry Street, Neath, 1945.

Residents of Llewellyn Street, Port Talbot, line up for the cameraman during its party to celebrate the Coronation of King George VI, 1937.

A group of Briton Ferry children gather for a birthday party – 1948 style.

There were plenty of tasty goodies to go round when residents of Brynglas Avenue, Cwmavon, celebrated VE Day in 1945.

Children of Olive Street, Aberavon, during their VE Day celebrations, 1945.

Neighbours from Cattle Street, Duck Street, Glamorgan Street, Castle Buildings, Castle Street and Russell Street, were all in attendance for this celebration at Cattle Street, Neath, held to commemorate the Festival of Britain, on August 28, 1951.

The official opening of Ynys Bowling Club, Velindre, Port Talbot, 1947.

A celebratory tea party held in Bethel Chapel, School Road, Crynant, to commemorate the Coronation of Queen Elizabeth II, 1953.

Mayoress of Port Talbot Mrs Richard Evans presents the prizes at a cake making competition organised in the town by the Wales Gas Board, on Wednesday, June 13, 1951. The winner was Mrs J.C. Rees, of Bridgend, who received a voucher for £10. Two Port Talbot women were runners up.

A celebration tea party at Roman Way, Neath to mark the Coronation of Queen Elizabeth II, 1953.

The Mayor of Port Talbot, Alderman Richard Evans, proclaims the accession of Queen Elizabeth II, after the death of her father, King George VI, 1952.

The Coronation carnival band organised by residents of Pendarvis Terrace, Aberavon, June, 1953.

Some of the children who attended a party at the Welfare Hall, Cimla, Neath, to celebrate the Coronation of Queen Elizabeth II, in June 1953.

Residents gather at Bryn Road, Mount Pleasant, Neath to celebrate the Coronation of Queen Elizabeth II, 1953.

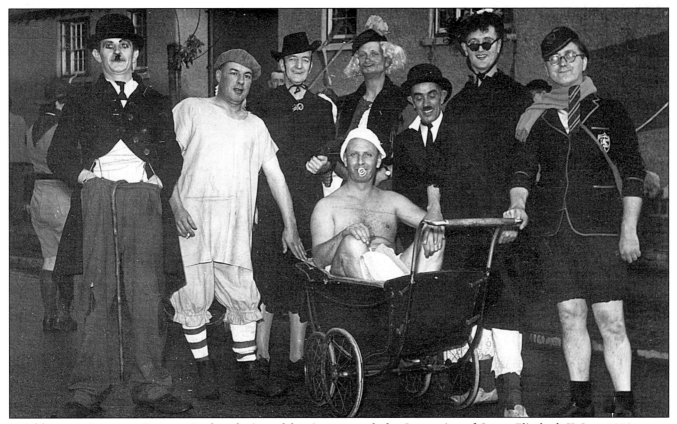

Neighbours at Sycamore Crescent, Baglan, during celebrations to mark the Coronation of Queen Elizabeth II, June 1953.

Children from Roman Way, Neath, all dressed up to celebrate the Coronation of Queen Elizabeth II, in June, 1953.

Residents of Pendarvis Terrace and Stair Street, Aberavon, celebrating the Coronation of Queen Elizabeth II, 1953. Rain on the day led to the party being held in a large garage behind Stair Street, owned by Mr B. Denby.

Residents – young and old – of Middleton Street, Briton Ferry, at the street party they held to celebrate the Coronation of Queen Elizabeth II, June, 1953.

Mothers and children of Old Cornwall Street – later Henshaw Street – Aberavon, at their Coronation Street Party, June 1953.

A Corpus Christi procession at St Joseph's Roman Catholic Church, Neath, 1956.

Members of Neath Methodist Church walk along Windsor Road during their annual Whitsun procession, 1956.

Coronation celebrations at Lingfield Avenue, Port Talbot, June, 1953.

Residents of Ruskin Avenue, Aberavon, celebrate the Coronation of Queen Elizabeth II, June, 1953.

Members of St David's Church Mothers, Union, Neath, take part in the annual Whitsun parade, 1958. They are pictured heading eastwards along the town's Windsor Road.

Members of the Welsh Guards prepare to head off on parade from the drill hall at Ynys Street, Port Talbot, 1953. The area later became Island Mews housing development.

Attending Neath Guide Fair on Thursday, May 16, 1963, was one of the last civic duties to be performed by Mayor of Neath, Alderman Ernie Molland, as he came to the end of his year of office. Pictured with him at the cake stall are his twin daughters who shared the role of mayoress for six months each.

A Whitsun walk at Cwmavon, 1961.

A presentation to Mr Bob Henry, manager of the National Assistance Board at Neath, on the occasion of his retirement, 1965.

On May 31, 1963, crowds lined the route as the Lord Mayor of London, Sir Ralph Perring took part in a parade through the streets of Port Talbot. Here his coach passes Bethany Square headed up by the City Marshall on horseback.

Celebration time for the landlord and landlady, Lee and Laura Davies, and regulars of The Greyhound Inn, Water Street, Neath, after winning the football pools, 1966.

Aber-Blaengwynfi carnival queen and her attendants, 1966.

Neath Borough Council refuse collectors took part in Cimla carnival in 1972 and won the shield for the best float.

Residents of Chapel Street, Blaengwynfi, at the village's Western Hotel during celebrations to mark the Investiture of the Prince of Wales, July, 1969.

Staff of John Owen & Co, iron and steel stockholders, Neath, at a dinner to mark the retirement of Alderman Ernie Molland, as director and company secretary, 1974.

Celebrations at Tirmorfa School, Sandfields, Port Talbot, to mark the Investiture of the Prince of Wales, July, 1969.

Pupils of Crynallt Primary School, Cimla, Neath, march across Cimla common dressed in costumes from around the world to celebrate World Day, 1985 at Cimla church hall.

Smiles all round from these residents of Western Avenue, Sandfields, Port Talbot, as they celebrate the Investiture of the Prince of Wales, 1969.

Peter Parker, chairman of the British Railways Board, unveils a plaque to open Neath's new railway station on March 6, 1978.

STEEL APPEAL

The towns of Neath and Port Talbot both have long associations with heavy metal industries, but the year 2002 is significant for Port Talbot in particular as it marks the 100th anniversary of the start of the town's association with steel making. The following pictures show some of the developments that helped turn it into one of biggest steel producing towns in the world. In November 2001, one of the world's worst steelmaking accidents occurred when Blast Furnace number five blew out while being tapped.

A number of workers were killed and many injured in the incident. When this book was being printed the plant's owners, Corus, were working to rebuild the furnace.

Going… going… gone. The old makes way for the new – demolition of stacks at the old Port Talbot steelworks to make way for new development during the mid 1930s.

The office of the personal assistant to W.F. Cartwright, managing director of the old Port Talbot steelworks, 1920s.

Construction work under way over countless acres for what was to become the Steel Company of Wales, Abbey Works, Port Talbot. This aerial view was taken in 1948.

An inside view of construction work under way at the rolling mill, Steel Company of Wales, Margam, 1948.

Inaugural Ceremony
at the Abbey Works of The Steel Company of Wales Limited
at which Their Majesties The King and The Queen
have graciously consented to be present.

The Chairman and Directors of The Steel Company of Wales
request the pleasure of the company of

The Worshipful the Mayor & Mayoress of Port Talbot

at Abbey Works, Port Talbot on Tuesday, July 17th, 1951
at 11·45 a.m. prior to luncheon at 12·45 p.m.

Informal Dress.
R.S.V.P. on enclosed card.

Sadly the deteriorating health of King George VI prevented him from fulfilling this appointment. Hugh Gaitskill, Chancellor of the Exchequer, took his place instead.

Guests arrived at the plant in fleets of private coaches specially hired for the task, on Tuesday, July 17, 1951.

Apprentices Colin Cokely, Norman Murray, Tudor Davies and Malcolm Dummer take a break from their labours at the steel plant in 1954.

Construction work alongside one of the huge blast furnaces at the plant, 1957.

Early work under way to construct the Bessemer plant. The picture was taken looking north-west towards the dolomite shop and converter bay, October 9, 1957.

The southern end of the cold mill extension viewed from one of the plants towering lighting platforms, 1957.

Workmen pause for a break outside the hot mill workshop, 1958.

Up, up and away –
work continues on
further extension
construction in
1957.

One of the many private Steel Company of Wales buses used to ferry staff around the plant and to and from their homes, 1959.

Installation of rolling mill equipment at the Steel Company of Wales, Abbey works, 1959.

This crane was a familiar sight as it worked alongside the Abbey Melting Shop. It is pictured during maintenance work, January, 1960.

One of the gearing rings used on the huge cranes that helped feed the Abbey Melting Shop with scrap being replaced, January, 1960.

An aerial view of the Steel Company of Wales Abbey Works, Port Talbot, 1962.

A retirement presentation to a member of staff at the central engineering shop, 1963.

Members of the works council at the British Steel Corporation Works, Port Talbot, as it was by now named, prepare for a trip to London, from Port Talbot general station, early 1970s.

Members of the works Council at BSC, Port Talbot, 1972.

Charging molten iron into one of the 300 ton converters at the Basic Oxygen Steelmaking plant at BSC's Port Talbot works, which was opened in 1976.

A view of the back of blast furnaces, from left to right, numbers one, two and three, taken from the Sinter Plant at BSC, Port Talbot.

TAKING A BREAK

Members of the Chapman family at a summer shop they ran near the sands at Jersey Marine, early 1930s.

The Chapman family pictured at their shop, one of a number near Jersey Marine sands, early 1930s.

A group of Port Talbot children – Ray, Frank and Ivor Speed – with their father and aunt on a day trip to Porthcawl, 1932. The picture was taken at Lock's Common, alongside an aircraft giving short sightseeing flights. It proved a major attraction. The older boys are wearing Port Talbot County School caps.

Members of Neath Methodist Church on a summer outing, 1953. The coach that carried them on their way was owned by Cooper's of Crynant, one of the first companies in the area to use radios in their coaches.

Members of staff from the Great Western Railway's Port Talbot Docks office on an outing to Brighton on June 6, 1936. They topped off the day with an evening's entertainment at a theatre where Max Miller was top of the bill.

A group of Neath railwaymen on a day out in the early 1950s.

Members of the Port Talbot Corps of the Salvation Army on a day trip to Porthcawl, late 1940s.

Employees of the Albion steelworks, Briton Ferry, on an annual outing – a trip around the Wye Valley, June, 1953.

Donkey rides on Aberavon Beach, early 1950s.

A group of family and friends from Neath on holiday at Hastings, August, 1956.

Cwmavon, Port Talbot, residents on a night out to a firework display at Coney Beach, Porthcawl, 1951.

Members of Neath Townswomen's Guild on a paddle steamer trip, 1957.

Ready for the off. A group of Cwmavon residents shortly before setting off on a trip to Blackpool illuminations, 1951.

Railwaymen from Neath pictured in Paris under the Eiffel Tower, on a trip to watch Wales play France at rugby, April, 1959.

Members of the staff of Thomas Bros bus company pictured outside the firm's Acacia Avenue, Sandfields, Port Talbot, garage before setting off for a day out in the mid-1950s.

These swing boats were a popular attraction on Aberavon Beach, in the 1950s. This picture was taken in August 1955.

Time to relax on the sands at Aberavon – deckchair style – in the late 1950s. Remember duffle bags?

There was always plenty to catch the eye when the September Fair arrived in Neath, for its annual visit as these two sisters and their dad discovered in 1962. The parrot and monkey were familiar props for the wandering street photographers.

The sea lion pool at Penscynor Wildlife Park, Cilfrew, Neath, 1975. The park is now a housing development.

Pupils of Sandfields Comprehensive School, Port Talbot, on a day trip to Tenby, 1960.

A visit to Big Pit, Blaenavon, Gwent, was the order of the day for these pupils of Crynallt Primary School, Cimla, Neath, in 1986.

STEAMING ON

Locomotive 3023 hauls a mixed freight train into Neath goods yard after bringing it down the valley in the 1950s.

A Paddington-bound express hurtles through Briton Ferry station, early 1950s.

Dyffryn Yard locomotive sheds, Taibach, Port Talbot, 1954. In their heyday they were a hive of railway activity. The Wildbrook housing estate now occupies the site. On the right hand side of the picture the busy coal sidings have also vanished to be overtaken by the needs of housing.

Locomotive *Evening Star* awaits its next turn of duty at Neath locomotive sheds. *Evening Star* was the last steam locomotive built at Swindon Railway works. Neath General Hospital can be seen in the background, early 1960s.

The workshop used by blacksmiths and coppersmiths at Neath locomotive shed, early 1960s.

Signalman Ben Thomas peers out of the window of the signal box at Neath locomotive depot, 1960. Alongside he can be seen among the many levers he and his colleagues were called upon to operate.

Locomotives pictured after taking on coal at the coaling stage, Dyffryn locomotive yard, Port Talbot, June 21, 1962.

Neath locomotive shed fitting staff, 1962.

A train steams through the infamous level crossing gates at Station Road, Port Talbot, June 11, 1962.

The last steam-hauled South Wales Pullman express passes through Penrhiwtyn as it heads for Paddington, 1963.

Locomotive fitters at work at Neath engine sheds, 1963.

A freight train climbs Pyle bank after leaving Port Talbot behind, June 22, 1963.

A coal train waits at Port Talbot station June 4, 1963. Margam Terrace can be seen in the background.

A burst of steam as locomotive 7248 emerges from Lonlas tunnel, Skewen, on the Swansea District line travelling from Llanelli, on July 27, 1963. The tunnel and line was built to speed up the progress of the Paddington to Fishguard boat train.

A mixed freight train passes the Evans Bevan playing fields at Baglan, on July 22, 1963. Baglan loop signal box can be seen in the background. The unmistakable poplar trees alongside the field dwarf the scene now.

Locomotive 48438 puts out a tremendous head of steam as it hauls a mixed goods train up the embankment past Neath Girls Grammar School, on December 14, 1963.

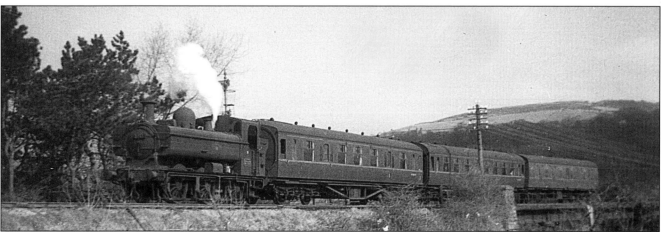

A locomotive and its three carriages on the Vale of Neath Railway line, April 4, 1964. The picture was taken near where Neath's Northern link road bridge was later built.

A passenger train, hauled by locomotive 4169, waits at Glynneath station on February 5, 1964.

A train prepares to leave Neath station for Port Talbot, on February 29, 1964.

A Neath Valley school train leaving Neath Riverside station, while behind, a double decker bus crosses the bridge into town, April 4, 1964.

A train of oil tankers trundles through Port Talbot during work to replace its general station, August 8, 1964.

The Chapel of Ease railway crossing on the line between Port Talbot steelworks and Dyffryn Yard locomotive sheds, early 1960s.

SCHOOL SNAPSHOTS

Central Infants School, Port Talbot, 1923.

Gnoll Girls School, Neath, 1916.

Pupils of Mountain School, Aberavon, at a summer camp Rhoose, Vale of Glamorgan, late 1930s.

Standard 1, Cwrt Sart Boys, School, Briton Ferry, 1923.

Abergwynfi Junior School, early 1930s.

Melin Elementary School, Neath, Christmas, 1939.

Cwmavon Boys, School, at a YMCA hostel, Cold Knap, Barry, 1936.

Standard 1 Cwrt Sart Infants School, 1930.

Standard IVA, Neath Boys Grammar School, 1939.

Pupils of Trefelin School, Velindre, Port Talbot at their summer camp at Pembrey, 1937.

Sandfields Girls, School, Lillian Street, Aberavon, 1950.

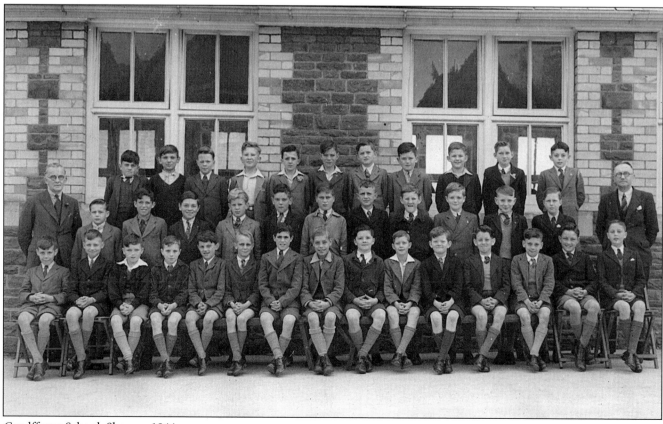

Coedffranc School, Skewen, 1944.

Miss Webb's class at Central School, Port Talbot, 1951.

Coedffranc Girls, School, Skewen, 1945.

Pupils of Sandfields, Junior School, Pendarvis Terrace, Aberavon, celebrate St David's Day, early 1950s.

Form IIIA, Neath Boys, Grammar School, 1949.

Pupils of Sandfields Senior School, Lillian Street, Aberavon, 1955.

Pupils of Alderman Davies, School, Neath at Ogmore summer camp, 1954.

Miss M. Murphy's class of girls at St Joseph's Infants School, Water Street, Port Talbot, 1955.

Children of the Wellfield Nursery, Neath, 1955.

Sandfields Senior School, Lillian Street, Aberavon, 1955.

Pupils of Cwrt Sart Junior School, on the playing fields at the school, 1955.

Mrs Sharp's class at Bryn Primary School, Port Talbot, 1956.

A group of pupils at Blaenhonddan Primary School, Bryncoch, Neath, 1958.

Pupils of St Joseph's Infants School, Water Street, Port Talbot, 1957.

A class of pupils at Ynysymaerdy School, Briton Ferry, 1959.

Pupils at Tirmorfa School, Sandfields, Port Talbot, 1958.

Girls at Alderman Davies, School, Neath, 1960.

Pupils of Tirmorfa School, Sandfields, Port Talbot, on St David's Day, 1958.

Form IV, Neath Grammar School, 1961.

Pupils at Glanafan School, Port Talbot, early 1960s.

Pupils of Standard 1, Brynhyfryd School, Briton Ferry, 1962.

The class of 1961 at Tirmorfa Junior School, Sandfields, Port Talbot.

Pupils at Crynallt Junior School, Cimla, Neath, 1972.

Children at Abergwynfi Junior School, 1966.

A group of pupils of Cefn Saeson Comprehensive School, Cimla, Neath, pictured with staff after receiving silver and bronze awards from the Duke of Edinburgh scheme, 1976.

Abergwynfi Junior School's Christmas production, 1966.

Form 5L Cefn Saeson Comprehensive School, Cimla, Neath, 1979.

Pupils of Tywyn School, Sandfields on St David's Day, March, 1978.

Mrs Bassett's class at
Ynysymaerdy Primary School,
Briton Ferry, 1979.

Class 6, Central Junior School,
Port Talbot, 1979.

Ysgol Gynradd Gymraeg, Castell Nedd – Neath Welsh School, 1980.

Pupils of Central Infants School, Port Talbot dressed in traditional costume for St David's Day, March 1, 1982.

Children of the nursery at the church of Saints Peter and Paul, Afan Valley Road, Cimla, Neath, 1982.

Pupils of the nursery at Neath Welsh Primary School, Woodland Road, Neath, 1986.

MOVING MEMORIES

Two wheels and plenty of foot power was all the transport young Lorrie Lewis of High Street, Abergwynfi, needed in the late 1920s.

The sailing vessel *Passatt* laid up at Port Talbot Dry Dock, 1947.

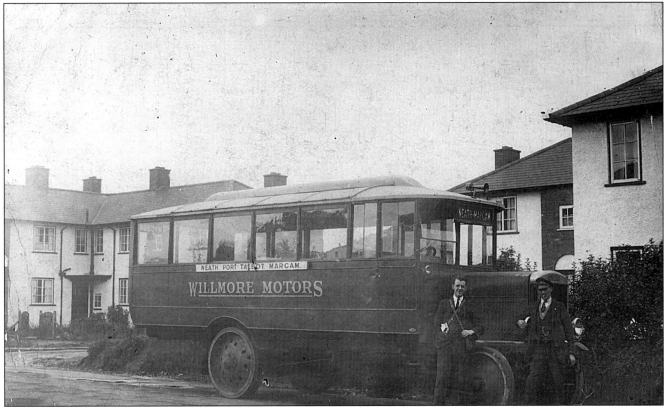

The driver and conductor of this Willmore Motors bus take a break before their next trip in mid-1920s. The service ran from Neath to Margam.

This open-top double decker was used by bus operators Wilmore Motors to carry passengers on its route from Neath to Margam, early 1920s.

Travellers setting off on the first pilgrimage to Lourdes from St Joseph's Roman Catholic Church, Water Street, Port Talbot in 1958. It was the centenary of Lourdes that year and the trip was memorable for the majority of those pictured boarding an aircraft at Rhoose – now Cardiff International – airport for its was their first flight.

Dan Perry and Horace James with the two taxis they ran at Skewen, 1935. The vehicles are seen here prepared for a wedding party.

These Leyland Tiger Cub buses operated by Thomas Bros, were among the many that transported thousands of passengers around Port Talbot in the late 1950s and '60s. They are pictured here picking up at Bethany Square.

A line-up of South Wales Transport coaches and their drivers at Victoria Gardens, Neath, late 1930s.

Thomas Bros. Buses at Seaway Parade, Sandfields, Port Talbot, early 1960s.

A Neath postman on parcel delivery duties in his Morris van, 1950.

The entrance to Port Talbot Docks, early 1960s.

This N&C Luxury Coaches vehicle collided with a lamp-post near, Lonlas, during 1952.

Port Talbot Docks, 1962.

A driver and his vehicle outside the South Wales Transport Company's Eastland Road depot, Neath, 1958.

For Julie Swansbury, of High Street, Abergwynfi, getting around in 1962 meant being wheeled along in a pushchair by sister Anne.

Some of the fleet of vans operated by wholesale confectioners Jenkins of Skewen in the 1950s.

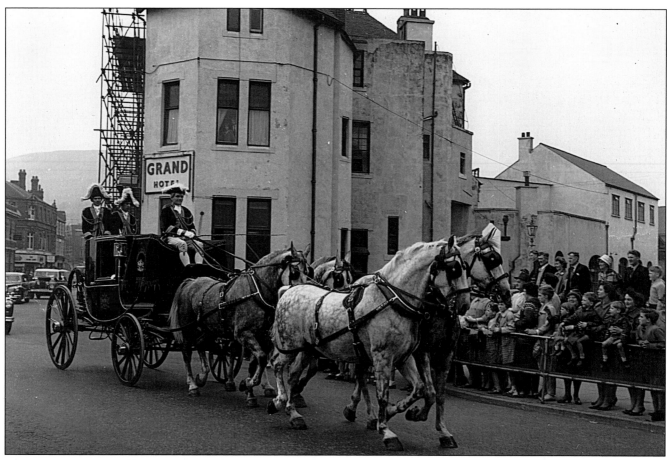

This was the coach used by Lord Mayor of London, Sir Ralph Perrin, when he visited Port Talbot on May 31, 1963. It is pictured passing the crowds that gathered at the entrance to Oakwood Lane, opposite the town's railway station.

Briton Ferry Works No.5 – *The Doll* – returning to the ironworks after dumping slag at Baglan., late 1950s.

A sad day for the merchant vessel *British Cavalier* as two tugs tow her the last few hundred yards to her final resting place at Thos. Ward's Giant's Grave ship-breaking yard at Briton Ferry, May 23, 1959.

Staff of Thomas Bros, Port Talbot, pose in the mid-1960s with some of the firm's summer best – an open top double decker and two coaches that carried thousands of the town's trippers far and wide.

Ready for the highway – three motorcyclists and their pillion passengers pose for a quick snap in the lane between High Street and Commercial Street, Abergwynfi, before setting off for a run in 1963.

A dredger at the South Wales Sand & Gravel Company wharf, on the River Neath at Briton Ferry, 1968.

One of the first vessels to tie up at the deep water jetty at Port Talbot tidal harbour, May 12, 1970.

In a final act of defiance the submarine Taciturn broke its moorings at Thos Ward's Giant's Grave, ship-breaking yard, Briton Ferry, and blocked the River Neath, when this picture was taken in 1972. The incident prevented vessels entering or leaving the Neath Abbey wharves. The submarine had arrived at the breakers on August 8, 1971.

A Steel Company of Wales ore carrier moored alongside Crown Wharf, Port Talbot docks, waiting for the tide after discharging her cargo, in 1971.

A winter's day at Victoria bus station, Neath, 1972.

These two lads would have had a long wait for a train at Neath General station on this snow-bound day in 1983.

Gone, but not forgotten – there can be few bus passengers in Neath who don't remember Creamline Services, of Tonmawr, operated by Randy Davies and his wife Esme. When all else failed you could guarantee that 'Randy's' would get through. This picture of one of the company's coaches turning from Windsor Road, Neath, into Alfred Street, on a snowy day in 1983 seems to prove the point.

MAKING IT WORK

Cwmafan Tinworks, steam mills group, early 1900s.

A team of workmen at Neath galvanising works, 1909.

The horses did much of the transport work for Taibach and Port Talbot Co-operative Society in the early 1900s.

Milk delivery rounds people and their floats outside Evans Alexandra Dairy, Winifred Road, Skewen, in the 1920s.

Workmen employed in building the road from Cymmer, Port Talbot, over the Bwlch Mountain to Treorchy, 1926.

The stationmaster and staff at Bryn Railway Station, mid-1930s.

Usherettes who worked at Briton Ferry Public Hall, 1928.

Captain Haydn Rees, centre, manager of Cefn Coed Colliery, Crynant, possibly preparing to descend to the shaft bottom in a huge bucket, 1930s.

Great Western Railway fitters at Port Talbot, mid-1930s.

Miners at Cefn Coed Colliery, Crynant, mid-1930s.

The face of Welsh mining in the 1950s. Ben Lewis of Abergwynfi.

Women employees at the Corona pop delivery depot at Courtland Place, Port Talbot, early 1950s.

These faces would have been familiar to many shoppers on Pullins greengrocery stall at Neath Market in the 1930s. On the left is Florrie Pullin, and on the right, her niece, Bella Taylor.

Canteen staff at the Steel Company of Wales, Port Talbot, 1950.

It was an interesting claim to fame. By the time Briton Ferry Boot Repair Centre celebrated its first anniversary on November 17, 1932, its members, drawn from the ranks of the local unemployed, had repaired no fewer than 2,148 pairs of boots.

Telegram boy messengers – Glen Rees, Bert Veale and Tommy Anderson – at Neath Post Office, 1937.

Mayoress of Port Talbot, Mary Evans, visiting the town's telephone exchange, 1952.

Employees at the Our Boys mineral water factory, Old Road, Briton Ferry, 1940.

Police officer Sidney G. Whomes, believed to be the last surviving member of Neath Borough Police force pictured on September 14, 1942.

A Neath postman on his rounds, 1950, and the same 'postie' on parcel duties, 1950.

Workers at Port Talbot Dry Dock, 1954.

Engineers at the N&C Luxury Coaches depot, James Street, Neath rebuilding vehicle number 549 from the bare chassis on an afternoon shift in 1952.

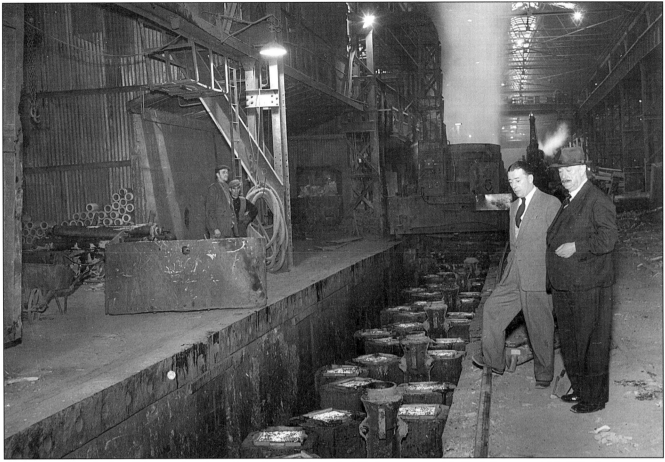

The pit road inside the Albion steelworks, Briton Ferry, early 1960s. Works managers Mr Pugh Bevan and Mr Kilby look at some freshly cast ingots, while in the background a furnace is being tapped.

Office staff of contractors William Press & Sons at their offices near the railway arches at Taibach, Port Talbot, mid-1960s.

Foreman Lyn Phillips and some of the paint shop girls at the Metal Spinning factory's, Millands Road, Neath factory, mid-1960s.

Some of the gang at Port Talbot Dry Dock, mid-1960s.

Staff of Tonna Children's, Hospital, Neath, 1961.

Editorial and advertising staff of the *Neath Guardian* newspaper, London Road, Neath, early 1970s.

Employees of the VLN plant at the Steel Company of Wales, Port Talbot, late 1960s.

Engineering and traffic staff of the South Wales Transport Company's Eastland Road, Neath, depot pictured before the last vehicle left before it was closed on February 28, 1971.

Barmaids at the British Legion Club, Blaengwynfi, February 16, 1974.

Some of the workforce of Holder Construction, Neath, on site, 1977.

A Christmas party held by staff of the DHSS Supplementary Benefits office, based at the Drill Hall, Port Talbot, 1978.

The last tap of K furnace at Duport steelworks, Briton Ferry – formerly the Albion steelworks – November 1978.

THE ENTERTAINERS

Ronnie Williams, Briton Ferry's famous boy drummer, at the age of six, November 1931. Ronnie who was born on May 1, 1925, died in 1985 and lived all his life in the town. More than one newspaper report of his concert exploits praised his coolness in the handling of his instruments and the accuracy of his playing.

Members of Aberavon's Seaside Usherettes jazz band, pictured with their shield after a championship success, 1935. The picture was taken in front of the now demolished Jersey Beach Hotel, on the seafront.

Madam Wynnie Richards Thomas's renowned Neath Concert Party, 1944. The group was well known for its concert for troops stationed in South Wales during the Second World War.

Velindre Highlanders Character Band, Port Talbot, which reached its competition peak in 1937, when this picture was taken.

Neath's Penry Denis All Girls Choir, 1950.

Members of Great Western Railway Social and Educational Union's Port Talbot Ladies, Choir, winners of the GWR Festival at Reading, 1937.

Members of the Calfaria Chapel Guild, Skewen, who performed the operetta *Playmates*, 1950.

Port Talbot's Great Western Railway Ladies, Choir, winners of the 1937 GWR Festival at Reading.

The cast of a play staged by members of St Catherine's Church, Melyncrythan, Neath, early 1950s.

Members of the cast of an operetta performed at Zion Church, Cwmavon, late 1940s.

The waste ground behind Mile End Row, Melyncrythan, Neath, was the ideal place for resident Sandra Morris to practice on her guitar, 1950s – particularly as she had nine younger brothers and sisters.

Members of Gibeon Church, Taibach, when they staged the pantomime *Robin Hood*, late 1940s.

St David's Church Sunday School, Neath, in fancy dress, Saturday, February 22, 1963.

Cwmavon YWCA members in Welsh costume during the late 1940s.

Côr Meibion Rhos Cwmtawe at their first annual concert, 1970.

Briton Ferry Amateur Operatic Society's production of *Sweethearts*, at The Gwyn Hall, Neath, 1970.

Brynbryddan Comedy Jazz Band, Cwmavon, 1954.

A scene from *Hello Dolly*, staged at The Gwyn Hall, Neath by Briton Ferry Amateur Operatic Society, 1971.

The swirl of the pipes drew quite a crowd when this band took part in a 1963 procession through the streets of Port Talbot town centre.

Beards galore for the male chorus members of Neath Amateur Operatic Society's 1973 production. Why? They were staging *Fiddler On The Roof* of course.

The Young Wives group of St Agnes Church, Port Talbot, in fancy dress, 1973.

The cast of the pantomime *Aladdin*, staged by pupils of Crynallt Primary School, Cimla, Neath, 1976.

Some of the Ladies Section of Taibach Rugby Club, Port Talbot, during a 1977 charity show.

The Grisettes – members of Neath Amateur Operatic Society – who took part in the November 1977 performance of *The Merry Widow*.

Cimla Jazz Band, marches across Cimla Common, Neath, 1980.

Aber-Blaengwynfi jazz band strides along high Street, Blaengwynfi, as it heads up a mid-1980s carnival.

Tonna Male Voice Choir, Neath, with its conductor and accompanist, 1982.

Three members of the Cefn Saeson Comprehensive School, Cimla, Neath, cast of the musical *Oliver*, 1982.

Some of the young cast members of the pantomime *Jack and the Beanstalk*, staged at the Afan Lido, Port Talbot, 1982.

Pupils of Neath Welsh Primary School who joined the cast of Cadoxton Opera Society's production of *Carmen*, 1986.

SPORTING SPIRIT

Cwrt Sart School sports team, Briton Ferry, 1928.

A motorcycle scramble, which was held in a field off Drummau Road, Skewen, late 1930s.

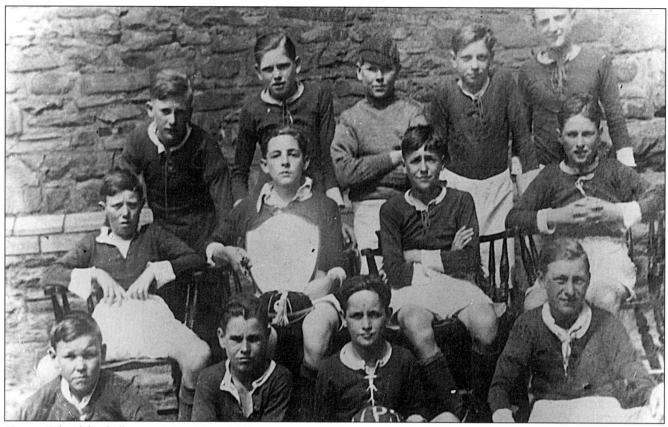

Vernon School football team, Briton Ferry, 1933.

A young Cwmavon rugby team from the late 1920s.

Briton Ferry Schools Football Association team, Welsh Shield runners-up season 1943-44.

The Bolshie football team at Cwmavon, late 1920s.

These were some of the girls who took part in a swimming gala at the Gnoll Park's first pond in the 1940s. The pond was a favoured swimming spot in the days before Neath had its own swimming pool.

This young Cwmavon rugby team was undefeated in its exploits during the 1929-30 season.

Neath Grammar School's athletic squad, 1949.

Ynys Juniors football team, Cwmavon, 1932-33.

The Gnoll School, Neath, cricket team which beat the town's grammar school team in the final of the Jack Kemp Cup competition, July, 1954. For winning the cup the lads were all given a free school dinner.

Cwmavon Youth rugby XV, 1948.

Briton Ferry Steel Bowls Club, late 1950s.

Darts players from the Crown Hotel, Water Street, Port Talbot, on a 1950 outing.

Gnoll School Rugby team, Neath, 1954.

Members of Ynys Bowls Club, Port Talbot, pictured with members of the Steel Company of Wales club before they met in competition, mid-1950s.

Neath Boys Grammar School athletic squad, 1959.

Members of the Steel Company of Wales Bowls Club, Port Talbot, 1957.

British Rail's Neath snooker team, early 1960s.

Dyffryn Comprehensive School's seven-a-side squad with teachers, which won the district schools, seven-a-side competition, 1973-74.

Neath Boys Grammar School athletics squad, 1960.

Cwmavon Boys Club football team, 1976.

Alderman Davies' Primary School, Neath, cricket XI, 1961.

The committee of Gwynfi Youth AFC, June 6, 1976.

Members of the Gnoll School, Neath, athletic team, 1962.

Presentation night at Gwynfi Youth AFC, Port Talbot, April 6, 1976.

Ynysygerwn Cricket Club, Neath, Youth XI, 1968.

This was the one that didn't get away! Keith Davies, of Dylan Crescent, Sandfields, with a huge cod caught fishing off Rhossili, 1981.

Giant's Grave Fishing Club, Briton Ferry, on a fruitful sea fishing expedition, 1969.

Tonmawr Cricket Club members at a celebration at the Jersey Beach Hotel, Aberavon, to celebrate winning their division in the Morgannwg Cricket League, November, 1982.

Blaenhonddan Primary School's rugby team, Bryncoch, Neath, 1973.

Dwryfelin Comprehensive School rugby team, Neath, 1976-77 season.

The swimming team at Ysgol Gymraeg Castell Nedd – Neath Welsh School – 1979.

Neath Boys Club soccer team, 1982-83 season.

The successful Neath YMCA gymnastics team, 1984.

Awards night at Cwmavon Schoolboys Football Club, Port Talbot, 1982.

Cefn Saeson Comprehensive School netball team, Cimla, Neath, 1985.